Career Advancement
Communication Strategies for Professional Growth

Table of Contents

Chapter 1. Introduction

In the thrilling and dynamic world of career progression, the ability to communicate astutely can propel your professional growth exponentially. Our Special Report, "Career Advancement: Communication Strategies for Professional Growth," offers an enlightening window into mastering this crucial skill. Whether you are just starting your career or are stuck in the corporate labyrinth with years of experience, this compendium offers judicious advice on proactively fostering beneficial relationships, presenting eloquently during meetings, and showcasing your expertise in a proficient way that validates your potential. Delve into a treasure trove of actionable insights, case studies, expert interviews, and much more to elevate your career. A radiant future awaits you, it's just one effective conversation away! Buy this special report today and embark on your journey towards seamless communication and rewarding career advancement.

Chapter 2. Understanding the Power of Effective Communication

Communication, in theory, is as simple as conveying your thoughts to another person via a medium. In reality, however, it extends far beyond that definition. Effective communication entails the ability to accurately and eloquently deliver your thoughts, feelings, or ideas in a way that prompts action, achieves solutions, or brings about desired change. It is a harmonious blend of art and science, mixing verbal and non-verbal cues, emotional intelligence, and situational awareness to elucidate messages in dynamic environments.

2.1. The Basics of Effective Communication

To grasp the concept fully, it is crucial to understand the basics of effective communication. It is made up of three components: the sender, message, and receiver. The sender conveys the message, and the receiver interprets it. Intricate as this process sounds, it only scratches the surface. Many factors contribute to the effectiveness of the communication, such as the sender's and receiver's perceptions, their background and experiences, and the context and medium of the communication.

Understanding the nuances that impact this process facilitates more effective communication. For instance, being aware of non-verbal cues, such as body language, can significantly improve your interaction. Gestures, facial expressions, and tone of voice can support or contradict verbal communication and often convey more than words alone.

2.2. Role of Emotional Intelligence in Communication

Emotional Intelligence (EI) is key in effective communication. It is the ability to understand, manage, and appropriately respond to emotions, both our own and others'. People with high EI tend to express their feelings in a manner aligned with their thoughts, and they are adept at empathising with and accurately interpreting others' emotions. This quality enhances communication, validating emotions and promoting a shared understanding. Learning and enhancing EI can markedly boost your proficiency in communication.

2.3. The Power of Active Listening

Active listening is an often overlooked aspect of communication. To be an effective communicator, one must also be an exceptional listener. This includes not only hearing the words spoken by others but truly understanding their message and emotional intent. The practice entails providing feedback, summarizing statements, avoiding distractions and interruptions, and expressing empathy. Enhancing your active listening skills can dramatically improve your overall communication prowess.

2.4. The Art of Concise Communication

While detailed communication is necessary in many scenarios, there is a distinct power in brevity. Clear, concise, and direct communication minimizes misunderstandings and respects others' time. It's essential to learn how to distil complex thoughts into understandable, succinct expressions without sacrificing crucial information. This ability is especially influential in time-sensitive or high-stakes environments such as business negotiations or mission-critical project meetings.

2.5. Non-verbal Communication: The Unsaid Language

While verbal interaction forms a large part of communication, non-verbal cues often carry the bulk of the message. Body language, facial expressions, eye contact, and even silence can speak volumes. Understanding non-verbal communication helps to create a more accurate picture of others' feelings and thoughts, facilitating deeper understanding and empathy.

2.6. The Impact of Effective Communication on the Workplace

In a professional context, effective communication is undeniably a precursor to success. It improves team collaboration, enhances efficiency, reduces misinterpretations, and strengthens relationships at every level of hierarchy. Organizations with robust communication systems enjoy greater employee engagement, higher satisfaction, and unsurprisingly, better performance and productivity.

2.7. Improving Communication Skills

Like any other skill, communication can be improved with conscious effort and practice. Enhancing listening skills, paying attention to non-verbal cues, seeking feedback, and being open to criticism are all significant methods of improvement. Investing time and energy into personal and professional development in this area is an investment worth making.

2.8. Conclusion

Understanding the power of effective communication is just the beginning. Translating this awareness into action requires practice, patience, and perseverance. Heightening your emotional intelligence, refining active listening skills, mastering concise communication, and interpreting non-verbal cues can all contribute to your overall proficiency. As you foster these skills, you will find inclusivity embedded within your conversations, leadership embraced in your dialogues, and success manifested in your career. You will reveal the true power of effective communication—an ability to inspire change.

Remember, this isn't merely about excelling in your career—it's about growth in every aspect of your life. Empower yourself with this information, and let effective communication be your guide toward a prosperous future.

Chapter 3. Mastering Verbal Communication for Professional Success

Verbal communication is the bedrock on which we build our professional relationships and demonstrate our expert knowledge. It permeates every aspect of our work lives, from phone calls and meetings to presentations and casual conversations. By mastering verbal communication, you equip yourself with the power to shape your professional image and leverage these interactions for career success.

3.1. Understanding the Basics

Language is more than the words we use; it is how we choose to use them. Certain words encourage cooperation and mutual respect, while others create distance and conflict. Understanding the importance of choosing the right words and presenting them in a respectful and positive manner forms the foundation of effective communal communication. Yet, it goes beyond that. Mastering the essence of verbal communication also involves understanding your audience, mastering the art of listening, and learning how to control and use your non-verbal cues in conjunction with your words.

3.2. The Art of Listening

Consider a scenario where you give a brilliant, fact-filled presentation, but then fumble when a colleague asks a question because you were lost in your own thoughts. Brilliant communication can be wasted if it's not paired with active listening. Here are some steps to enhance your listening abilities:

- **Pay Attention**: Being truly present in the conversation, focusing on the speaker and tuning out distractions can help you absorb information more effectively.

- **Refrain from Interrupting**: Let the speaker finish their thought before sharing yours. This shows respect for their ideas.

- **Follow-up Questions**: Ask clarifying or confirming questions. It lets the speaker know that you're engaged in the conversation.

3.3. Bridging the Gap with Non-Verbal Cues

Over 90% of communication is non-verbal, which means our actions often speak louder than our words. This refers to our body language, facial expressions, eye contact, tone of voice, and even our silence. When these non-verbal cues match up with the words we're saying, they increase trust, clarity, and rapport. Keep your posture open, maintain steady eye contact, modulate your tone to keep it friendly and respectful, and be aware of how the other person is reacting to ensure your message is perceived the way you intend it to be.

3.4. The Power of Precision and Clarity

Be concise and clear in your communication. This not only saves time but also prevents misinterpretations. Eliminate jargon when not necessary, avoid ambiguous language, and aim to get your point across in the simplest way possible. Prudent use of language boosts our credibility and fosters efficient communication.

3.5. Advocating Your Ideas Effectively

Whether you're proposing a new strategy, negotiating a deal, or merely voicing your thoughts in a meeting, an integral part of professional success hinges on how effectively you advocate your ideas. Remember to:

- **Know Your Audience**: Tailor your communication depending on who your listeners are – their backgrounds, their expertise level, their interests. This shows respect towards them and make your idea more appealing.

- **Build a Strong Case**: Back your idea with logic, data, and relevance. This lends credibility to your thoughts.

- **Stay Open to Feedback**: This encourages a culture of collaboration and shows that you value the opinions of others.

3.6. Handling Tough Conversations

Difficult conversations may involve delivering bad news, addressing performance issues, or resolving conflicts. They are challenging but often inevitable in professional life. To handle them with grace:

- **Prepare Ahead**: Know the points you want to address, anticipate reactions, and think about possible solutions.

- **Stay Calm and Composed**: Control your emotions and avoid getting personal.

- **Create a Constructive Atmosphere**: Encourage dialogue and mutual problem-solving.

Conclusively, mastering verbal communication in professional life is a calculated exercise of understanding, experimenting, learning and evolving. We have a natural capacity to speak and make ourselves understood, but it takes effort and conscious practice to do so effectively within the diverse and dynamic work environments of today. The benefits are vast: improved relationships, boosted credibility, seized opportunities, and, ultimately, the success and growth in your career.

[NOTE: The use of bullet points is in line with the Asciidoc syntax. Also, the '===' marker has been used to signify subheadings, again in alignment with Asciidoc conventions.]

Chapter 4. Unlocking the Potential of Non-Verbal Cues

While the world is chattering incessantly, encoding, decoding messages every nanosecond, a captivating and equally essential aspect of communication remains predominantly subdued. This vital feature is non-verbal communication, the subtler and more nuanced form of human interaction. By focusing on this, professionals can unlock reservoirs of potential and elevate their careers to extraordinary heights.

4.1. Understanding Non-Verbal Cues

Imagine a situation where you are delivering a vital presentation. Your sentences are eloquently structured, your message is crisp, yet your audience seems disengaged. The issue does not lie with your verbal communication but rather with your non-verbal cues. From our facial expressions to our body movements, we are constantly emitting signals that affect how others perceive our messages. Understanding these non-verbal cues can profoundly enhance our communication prowess.

Non-verbal communication comprises various elements like facial expressions, body movements and posture, eye contact, gestures, tone of voice, and even our physical space or environment. All these elements play a significant part in conveying information and manipulating the context of the conversation.

4.2. The Power of Facial Expressions

Facial expressions are often the first visible signs of our thoughts and emotions. Seemingly small cues, like the raising of an eyebrow or the furrowing of the brow, can speak volumes about what we are feeling.

Mastering your facial expressions is paramount to establishing emotional connections and maintaining the overall tone of the conversation.

In professional settings, ensure that you maintain a positive and approachable expression. A simple smile can evoke sentiments of trust and cooperation, thereby fostering better professional relationships.

4.3. Body Movements and Posture: Your Silent Orator

Just as how we say something can often be more important than what we say, the way we carry ourselves can cast a significant impact that our words might fail to deliver. Standing tall, not only boosts your self-confidence but also commands authority and respect.

Mirroring someone's body language can also create a sense of rapport and understanding. However, do it subtly and be sure it's not taken as mimicry, which could lead to misunderstandings.

4.4. Eye Contact: A Key to Connection

Eye contact, when used correctly, can become a powerful tool in non-verbal communication. In most cultures, steady eye contact conveys sincerity, attentiveness, and transparency. It is instrumental in forming connections and practicing active listening.

However, too much eye contact can come across as intimidating. An optimal balance needs to be maintained to ensure a comfortable and productive communication experience.

4.5. Vocal Elements: The Unsaid Truths

Non-verbal cues are not limited to silent gestures. The tone, pitch, and speed of your voice can significantly alter your message's impact. A confident, steady tone can signal command and assertiveness, whereas a high-pitched rapid tone could showcase nervousness or uncertainty.

By understanding the potential resting in these vocal elements, you can modulate your voice according to the situation, consequently facilitating effective communication.

4.6. Personal Space: A Subliminal Message

The physical space we maintain from others, our environment, and how we arrange it, all hold subtle cues about our preferences, style of work, and our level of comfort. Respecting the personal space of others, organizing a conducive environment for communication are important elements of non-verbal communication.

An effectively arranged meeting space can foster clarity, focus, and openness, while disruptive surroundings might lead to miscommunication and discontent.

Non-verbal communication is a potent tool, like a silent language that everyone understands but often underestimates. By mastering these cues, you can unlock potential beyond verbal barriers, opening more doors towards career advancement. Remember, effective non-verbal communication not only supplements your verbal communication but can sometimes replace it entirely. In the corporate labyrinth, such competence can make the difference between being just another employee and a successful professional.

Chapter 5. Navigating Difficult Conversations with Ease

Navigating difficult conversations is an unavoidable aspect of any business setting. It's when stakes are high, opinions vary, and emotions start to run that we need to handle with care. But how can we accomplish this with tact and ease? It's all about the strategies, techniques, and understanding of human psychology.

5.1. Recognizing Difficult Conversations

The first step in navigating difficult conversations is knowing when you're in one. Everyone has experienced a difficult conversation at work. These ranges from providing critical feedback to an underperforming team member, negotiating salary or project deadlines, dealing with personal conflict in your team, or advocating for yourself when you feel overlooked or undervalued. In these situations, you might feel your heart rate increase, your palms sweat, or feel emotionally drained. These physiological reactions are signs that you are in a high-stakes conversation.

Awareness is the first step to effectively navigating such encounters. When you recognize these signs, you can consciously switch from impulsive reactions to a more strategic approach.

5.2. The Foundation: Emotional Intelligence

Emotional intelligence (EI) plays a significant role when it comes to dealing with challenging conversations. EI is the ability to understand and manipulate your own and others' emotions effectively. Individuals who excel in EI tend not to avoid difficult discussions but rather approach them with the right set of skills and mindset. They are adept in empathetic listening, maintaining their composure, acknowledging others' feelings, and articulating their viewpoints respectfully and assertively.

Building your emotional intelligence can start with simple steps like paying attention to your emotional reactions, practicing empathy, or even seeking feedback on your interaction with others. As you refine this skill set, you will become more competent in approaching challenging dialogues.

5.3. Preparing for the Conversation

One key to successfully navigating difficult conversations is preparation. Your primary goal should not merely be to survive the conversation, but to cultivate mutual understanding and, if possible, arrive at a resolution that is mutually satisfactory.

As a first step, clarify your intent in your mind. This will give your conversation direction and purpose. If you're providing feedback to a team member, for instance, your intent may be to help them improve their performance.

Next, anticipate the other person's response to your points. Ponder upon their perspectives and consider the emotional dynamics at play. By understanding their probable reactions, you are better prepared to address them constructively.

5.4. Conducting the Conversation

Maintaining calmness during the dialogue is crucial as it sets the tone. Start by stating your intention clearly and honestly. Frame your message in a way that focuses on observations and impacts rather than the individual's personality.

Furthermore, nailing the art of delivering feedback is essential to converse effectively. Constructive feedback is best delivered using the "sandwich method:" positive statement - constructive criticism - positive statement.

Practice active listening. Allow the other person to voice their views without interrupting. Display empathy towards their feelings and perceptions. This can demonstrate respect and may diffuse tension in the conversation.

5.5. Managing Impacts After the Conversation

The impact of a difficult conversation extends beyond the dialogue itself. Therefore, it's imperative to debrief and follow up after the conversation. Reiterate key points that were discussed, establish a plan of action, agree on next steps, and document them if necessary.

Also, take time to reflect on the conversation. What went well? What could be improved for future similar circumstances? This reflection is critical to your continual learning process in navigating tough conversations.

5.6. Cultivating a Positive Culture

Navigating difficult conversations in the workplace isn't solely about individual capability. It's also about fostering an environment that encourages open, honest communication. Cultivating a culture where feedback and differing opinions are seen as opportunities for growth, rather than points of conflict, is a winning strategy.

Adopting these strategies will empower individuals to navigate difficult conversations with ease and finesse. And with this skill in your repertoire, you will not only be able to overcome obstacles but also enhance your relationships at work, thereby bolstering your career progression.

Chapter 6. Developing Emotional Intelligence for Workplace Relationships

Emotional intelligence is often recognized as a vital tool for fostering successful relationships in the workplace. Broadly defined, it refers to the ability to recognize, understand, and manage our own emotions, as well as the capacity to recognize, understand and influence the emotions of others.

6.1. Understanding Emotional Intelligence

Understanding emotional intelligence is the first step toward developing it. Author and psychologist, Daniel Goleman, broke it down into five key areas: self-awareness, self-regulation, motivation, empathy, and social skills.

Self-awareness:

It refers to the ability to recognize one's own emotions, strengths, weaknesses, drives, values, and goals and recognize their impact on others. To improve self-awareness, one can begin by taking time each day to reflect on one's emotions and analyze the situations that triggered them.

Self-regulation:

This pertains to controlling or redirecting disruptive emotions and impulses. To improve self-regulation, one must understand the triggers and learn to pause and think before reacting impulsively. Regular exercise, adequate sleep, and proper nutrition can also aid self-regulation.

Motivation:

Self-motivated individuals are capable of pursuing their goals with energy and persistence. To enhance motivation, establish and write down clear personal and professional goals. Then regularly track progress and celebrate successes, however small.

Empathy:

Empathy is understanding other people's feelings and responding accordingly. Practice active listening, where you focus fully on the speaker, and try to understand their perspective. This can help enhance empathy.

Social Skills:

Competence in managing relationships, building networks, and the ability to inspire and influence others describes one's social skills. To enhance them, seek feedback, learn from mistakes, and strive for continuous improvement.

6.2. The Role of Emotional Intelligence in Workplace Relationships

In the realm of workplace relationships, emotional intelligence is critically important. People with high emotional intelligence often have strong working relationships because they can understand and relate to their colleagues' feelings. They are also astute in managing their emotions, which allows them to handle stress, provide feedback, espouse teamwork, and navigate conflicts more proficiently.

Mitigating conflict is another area where emotional intelligence shines. Recognizing and addressing potential conflict sources before they fester and escalate is a valuable skill. This includes understanding underlying emotional currents running within the team and intervening with conflict resolution strategies as needed.

6.3. Techniques for Enhancing Emotional Intelligence

Building emotional intelligence is not an overnight task, it's an ongoing endeavor. Some techniques that can be instrumental in nurturing emotional intelligence include:

Mindfulness:

Regularly practicing mindfulness or meditation can help improve all five components of emotional intelligence. When we are more aware of our emotions and thoughts, we can better manage and direct them towards positive outcomes.

Self-reflection:

Take time to reflect on your emotional responses. Understand what triggers strong emotional reactions and consider different response strategies. Keeping an emotion journal can aid self-reflection dramatically.

Seek Feedback:

To grow, we must understand our areas of strength and development. Seeking feedback on your emotional behavior will offer you insights that may not be apparent to you.

Practice Empathy:

Make a conscious effort to understand others' perspectives. During conversation, try to get into their shoes and respond accordingly.

6.4. Emotional Intelligence and Leadership

In leadership, emotional intelligence is often the difference between good and average. Leaders with high emotional intelligence can identify the emotions of their team members, empathize with their situations, and manage their team in a way that inspires and motivates them.

Such leaders are adept at managing their own emotions too. They can maintain a balanced emotional state even in high-pressure situations, which helps them take rational decisions and sets a positive tone for the team.

In conclusion, investing in enhancing your emotional intelligence has significant benefits, especially within the workplace. It can foster stronger relationships, mitigate conflict, and improve overall productivity. So whether you're a leader, an employee or somewhere in between, developing emotional intelligence can help you in strengthening workplace relationships, thereby propelling not just your own, but also the collective progression of your team.

Chapter 7. Writing for Success: Emails, Proposals, and Reports

The ease of your professional ascent is in tandem with the proficiency of your writing skills - granting you greater credibility, improved interpersonal relationships, and enhanced influence in decision-making processes. This chapter embarks on a journey of mastering such indispensable techniques as Email writing, Proposal drafting, and reporting.

7.1. Understanding the Essentials

Effective written communication starts at the understanding of the fundamentals. Contrary to popular belief, proficient business writing isn't always about utilizing convoluted jargon and intricate language.

1. Clarity: Keep your content clear by avoiding any unnecessary complexity. Defining your objective early in your communication provides your readers with the context they need to correctly interpret your message.

2. Conciseness: While it's crucial to give a full picture, unnecessary verbosity can dilute the strength of your message. Know what to include and what to omit; cut the fluff.

3. Active Voice: Using the active voice, primarily, facilitates clear comprehension. Passive sentences often sound dull, or involve more words than required.

7.2. Mastering Emails

Email communication stands as an invincible pillar of professional communication. Balancing formality with the readability is vital.

1. Subject Line: Capture the essence of your message in the subject line, making it relevant and succinct.

2. Opening Salutation: Begin your mails professionally. A "Dear [First Name]," usually suffices unless the relationship is more formal.

3. Body: Ensure your email's body consists of clear, concise, and astutely structured content, strengthening your message.

4. Closing: An appropriate, polite sign-off followed by your name ends your email on a charming note.

7.3. Crafting Successful Proposals

Drafting compelling proposals is paramount in securing client agreements, or receiving project approval. These documents project your or your organization's caliber.

1. Executive Summary: Position this at the beginning of your proposal. Your executive summary should highlight your proposition's unique selling point.

2. Problem Statement: Identify and describe the problem that your proposal aims to solve, ensuring the reader aligns with your perspective.

3. Solution: Outline your proposal in a way that presents it as an optimal solution to the problem. Use data, case studies, or forecasts to support your solution.

4. Conclusion: Cement your proposal with a robust resolution, reminding your reader of the key issues and how your proposal alleviates them.

5. Follow-Up: Leave a path to action. A specific timeline, contact information, or an invitation for queries encourages an active response.

7.4. Reporting for Progress

Reports are systematic and well-organized documents that help you to deliver necessary information in an understandable manner. Following are the essential components that compile an effective report:

1. Introduction: Introduce your report, setting the tone, establishing the topic, and providing necessary context.

2. Methodology: Explain the methods you used to gather your data. This allows others to assess the reliability and validity of your sources.

3. Findings: Present your findings in a logical sequence. Use charts, graphs, or tables in this section to enhance clarity.

4. Discussions: Interpret your results. Compare them with your predictions and with other similar studies.

5. Conclusions: Distill the essence of your findings into a succinct conclusion.

6. Recommendations: Based on your findings, suggest further actions. These recommendations provide a pathway for future actions.

Writing for success in a professional milieu requires diligent efforts, but the rewards far outweigh the toil. With the right kind of practicing and the application of the techniques outlined above, you will find yourself becoming an articulate writer in no time.

Chapter 8. Public Speaking: Command the Room

Achieving command over public speaking is a vital part of advancing in the professional world. In public speaking, your task is to inspire, inform, convince, or enlighten an audience. The better you get at it, the higher your chances of impressing your superiors and moving up the company ladder.

8.1. Crucial Aspects of Commanding the Room

Fundamental Factors

1. Content: What you say is as crucial as how you say it. Ensure your material is insightful, credible, and corroborated by facts.

2. Delivery: Articulation, pronunciation, tone, pauses, pitch, emphasis on key points – they all contribute to the delivery of a message.

3. Body Language: How you hold yourself on stage communicates a great deal. Stand tall, make eye contact, use appropriate gestures for emphasis.

4. Engagement: Engage the audience, maintain eye contact, ask rhetorical questions, encourage participation.

5. Attire: Dress appropriately for the occasion and audience. It sends a message of your regard for them and the event.

8.2. Understanding the Nerves

The fear or anxiety associated with public speaking – often referred to as Glossophobia – isn't unusual. Many people experience this, worrying they might forget their lines, fumble over words, or bore the audience. But nerves can help boost you, keeping you on your toes and maintaining a level of alertness necessary for an exceptional performance.

Four main strategies to manage nerves:

1. Acknowledge the nerves, and remember that even the most experienced speakers feel apprehension.

2. Preparation minimizes anxiety. Know your content inside out, arrive early, familiarize yourself with the venue.

3. Visualization techniques can reduce stress by imagining yourself commanding the room confidently.

4. Deep breathing or mindfulness exercises can help calm your mind and body before the event.

8.3. How to Prepare for a Public Speaking Event?

Effective Preparation Strategies

1. Identify the Purpose: Understand why you are speaking and what you should achieve.

2. Know your Audience: Tailor your speech according to their needs and expectations.

3. Structure your Speech: Build a clear, cohesive structure with an introduction, body, and conclusion.

4. Rehearse: Practice speaking aloud, using body language and visual aids as you would during the actual event.

5. Feedback: Use feedback from rehearsal to refine your speech.

8.4. Effective Delivery Techniques

A compelling delivery is what separates a good speaker from a great one. The tone of voice, pace, use of silence, body language – all play an essential part.

Recommendations for Effective Delivery

1. Project Your Voice: Ensure everyone in the room can hear you.

2. Use Pauses: Leverage pauses for emphasis and to allow your audience to absorb your message.

3. Show Passion: Display enthusiasm and emotion about your topic.

4. Display Appropriate Body Language: Be mindful of your gestures, posture, and facial expressions.

5. Eye Contact: Engage with your audience by keeping eye contact.

8.5. Engaging with the Audience

Audience engagement is necessary for ensuring your message resonates with your listeners. Engagement involves building a connection with your audience through interaction. This can be accomplished by asking questions, sharing personal experiences, using humor, or letting the audience participate in a brief activity.

8.6. Learning from the Best

Numerous speakers have left a mark on the world with their public speaking skills. Study their techniques, how they structure their content, their tone, body language, timing, and how they connect with the audience. Famous public speakers can offer great pointers on how to command a room.

8.7. Continuous Improvement

Public speaking is an art that improves with practice. Even the most accomplished speakers continue to learn and polish their abilities. Gathering feedback after each speaking event, reflecting on your performance, and acting upon the received feedback is vital to continuous improvement and long-term success in commanding the room.

In conclusion, commanding the room during public speaking isn't something that happens overnight. It is a skill honed over time, with patience, preparation, practice, and a desire to improve continually. Step into the spotlight with confidence – a powerful way to advance in your career.

Chapter 9. Networking and Building Fruitful Relationships

The ability to forge and maintain strong professional relationships is a critical ingredient in the recipe for career success. Networking isn't just about attending industry events or making connections on LinkedIn. It requires a deliberate and strategic approach, underpinned by interpersonal skills, patience, and authenticity.

9.1. Defining Networking and Its Importance

No professional can work in isolation. Our complex, interconnected world necessitates bustling networks of relationships for advice, collaboration, and mentorship. Networking can be defined as the active process of creating, maintaining, and leveraging professional associations. It helps discover opportunities, obtain guidance, uncover ideas, and receive support to fuel your career growth.

From job hunting to business development or knowledge exchange, a sturdy network serves as your compass in the professional wilderness. It helps you stay informed about industry trends, gain unique insights, and access opportunities invisible to outsiders.

9.2. Understanding Relationship-Building

Now that we've established the importance of networking, let's delve into the art of building relationships. It's not about collecting business cards or racking up LinkedIn connections by the hundreds.

It's about building substantive relationships that bring mutual benefit.

1. **Sincerity** is at the core of any fruitful relationship. Approaching people with hidden agendas or self-centered motives will only breed distrust.

2. **Active listening** shows genuine interest and creates grounds for mutual respect.

3. **Consistency** in communication keeps you on others' radars and strengthens ties.

4. **Empathy and authenticity** help you understand others' perspectives better and foster honest, respectful relations.

9.3. Mastering the Art of Small Talk

Believe it or not, small talk - the informal chit-chat about non-controversial topics - is an important stepping stone to deeper, more meaningful conversations. Here are some tips:

1. Be aware of cultural nuances – what's acceptable in one culture could be a snag in another.

2. Ask open-ended questions to show interest and invite conversation.

3. Share just enough about yourself to stimulate reciprocal sharing.

4. Be attentive, responsive, and empathetic.

9.4. Building Your Personal Brand

The way you represent yourself professionally, both online and offline, plays a crucial role in networking. Your personal brand is more than your job title - it encompasses your work ethics, interests, values, and perceptible contribution to your field of expertise. Here are strategies to build an influential personal brand:

1. **Online Presence:** Present optimized profiles on professional platforms like LinkedIn, showcasing your abilities, achievements, and recommendations.

2. **Thought Leadership:** Regularly share your insights, experiences, and knowledge via blog posts or commenting on pressing issues in your domain.

3. **Consistency:** Ensure that your online persona and your real-life identity harmoniously resonate.

9.5. Leveraging Social Media for Networking

Social media platforms can be invaluable tools for networking if used strategically. Share useful content, join relevant groups, participate in discussions, and you're likely to attract likeminded professionals. Remember to behave professionally, though, and avoid sharing inappropriate or offensive content that may tarnish your image.

9.6. Networking in Professional Events

Attending industry-specific events offers a ripe opportunity to meet and interact with people who can potentially influence your career. But remember:

1. Do thorough research about the event, attendees, and their backgrounds to navigate smoothly.

2. Craft a succinct, compelling self-introduction.

3. Practice active listening and engage meaningfully.

9.7. Cultivating Relationships for the Long Term

Networking isn't a one-time task that you can check off your to-do list. It's a long-term commitment that involves nurturing and maintaining relationships. Regularly engage with your network through emails, calls, messages, or meetings. Remember, the objective of networking is not to have the greatest number of connections, but to build substantial relationships that enrich your professional journey.

Remember that networking and building relationships can feel arduous at times, but the payoffs are bountiful. The relationships you cultivate now will serve as stepping stones in your path to career success in the long run. So, step out of your comfort zone, connect, and converse – you never know where the next conversation will lead you!

Chapter 10. Managing Conflicts for Optimum Outcomes

The professional world is a complex tapestry of personalities, goals, and pressures. At times, these can create an environment ripe for conflicts. However, effective conflict management can transform potentially disruptive situations into opportunities for growth, collaboration, and innovative problem-solving.

10.1. Understanding Conflict

Conflict can stem from several sources in the workplace. It might arise from miscommunication, differing goals and objectives, contrasts in personalities, or competition for resources. Understanding the nature and the source of the conflict is the first step to managing it effectively.

There are basically five conflict management styles: avoidance, accommodation, compromise, competition, and collaboration. Each of these strategies has its own merits and demerits, and the best choice often depends on the specific context and the relationships of the parties involved.

10.2. Building a Communication Bridge

When engaged in a dispute, taking a step back to understand the other party's viewpoint is critical. Encourage open and respectful communication. Express your perceptions and feelings in a non-defending and non-blaming way, employing active listening skills to ensure each party feels heard and understood.

An example of this approach is using the "I" statements instead of "You" statements. Saying "I feel frustrated when deadlines are missed" is better and less accusing than saying "You are always missing deadlines." This affirms your feelings without directly blaming the counterpart.

10.3. Conflict Resolution Models

Several models for conflict resolution exist, but perhaps the most known and effective is the Thomas-Kilmann Instrument, based on the aforementioned five conflict-handling styles. Consider the most appropriate approach for your situation. Although some conflicts might require a competitive or compromise-style resolution, the ultimate goal is often to reach collaboration, wherein everyone's needs are met and mutual respect is maintained.

Another model is the Interest-Based Relational (IBR) approach to conflict resolution. It respects the individual needs of each party, ensures the process is fair, and promotes maintaining the relationship of the conflicting parties. Remember, in most professional settings, you will continue to interact with your colleagues post-conflict, making relationships of paramount importance.

10.4. Turning Conflict into Collaboration

Transforming a contentious situation into a collaboration begins with changing your mindset about the conflict. Instead of seeing it as a problem, view it as an opportunity to create a mutually satisfactory solution.

One useful technique is brainstorming possible resolutions. This encourages collaboration and the understanding that you are working together to combat the issue rather than each other.

Remember to affirm each suggestion. This doesn't mean you have to agree with each proposal, but rather that you appreciate the effort and the intention to find a mutual solution. This promotes a sense of teamwork and unity.

10.5. Navigating Cultural and Personality Differences

Workplaces are increasingly diverse, creating a melting pot of cultures, perspectives, and ways of working. Conflicts can arise from these differences if not managed well.

Being culturally intelligent and sensitive can help you navigate these differences successfully. It's about understanding other's viewpoints and being respectful of their values, even when they diverge from your own.

Similarly, understanding different personality types can aid in managing conflict. Certain personality types may clash more than others. For instance, a highly structured individual may conflict with a more flexible, creative peer. Understanding these dynamics can create an effective conflict resolution strategy.

10.6. Embracing the Growth Opportunities in Conflict

Conflict, undoubtedly, can be stressful and unwanted. However, it often brings about opportunities for personal and professional growth. It can spark creativity in problem-solving, improve communication and interpersonal skills, enhance understanding, and provide valuable insights into how your team works.

By learning to handle workplace conflicts effectively, you can turn these potential stressors into powerful catalysts for individual and organizational growth. This enriches your career advancement and quality of work-life. Deft conflict management is an essential component of your success toolkit, one that empowers you to catalyze every disagreement or dispute into a propellant for progress.

Chapter 11. Communication Strategies for Career Advancement: A Wrap Up

Having traversed the extensive terrain of efficacious communication strategies aimed at propelling career advancement, it's time to consolidate our insights. We've taken on a detailed examination of various strategies, deployed both theory and practical examples, and we've delved into expert advice and case studies. In this wrap-up, we shall revisit key themes, distill fundamental takeaways, and ensure that you are perfectly equipped to navigate professional dialogues with poise and confidence. Let's begin...

11.1. Comprehensive Understanding of Communication

Remember, at its core, communication is about exchanging thoughts, ideas, and information effectively. It's a two-way process, involving not just speaking, but also listening, and it extends to non-verbal exchanges, body language, tone of voice, and even the subtext of what is unsaid.

There's a diverse range of communication methods to remember; verbal (both in-person and over the phone), written (emails, reports), visual (graphs, charts), and non-verbal (body language, tone). Each has its strengths and weaknesses and is appropriate for different situations.

Effective communicators master these various forms, tune into the needs of the situation at hand, and adjust their methods accordingly. So reflect on your current strengths and areas for improvement across these diverse communication forms, and set yourself goals for honing each one.

11.2. The Power of Emotional Intelligence

A frequent theme in our discussions has been emotional intelligence – the ability to understand, interpret and respond to the emotions of yourself and others. It's widely recognized as an indispensable part of effective communication, and for good reason.

Emotional intelligence enables empathic understanding, fostering stronger, more genuine connections. This leads to productive relationships based on trust and respect. Furthermore, emotional intelligence allows for more efficient conflict resolution, facilitating open dialogues and compromise.

11.3. Communication and Relationship Building

Relationships are the bedrock of any career progression, and effective communication is the glue that binds them. Networking with peers, maintaining positive rapport with supervisors, and fostering a conducive work environment with subordinates all hinge on this crucial skill.

Remember to use targeted communication strategies to create lasting relationships. Leverage active listening and empathy to understand their needs and perspectives. Regular feedback sessions and open dialogues pave the way for trust-enriched relationships.

11.4. The Art of Persuasive Communication

Persuasive communication is an art. We've stressed the need to craft messages that appeal not just to the logic, but also to the values, beliefs, and emotions of the listener.

Remember Aristotle's ethos, pathos, and logos triumvirate. Establish credibility (ethos) through genuine behavior and evident expertise, emotionally connect with your audience (pathos) using carefully considered language, and use logical arguments and evidence (logos) to solidify your stance.

11.5. Public Speaking and Presentation Skills

Never underestimate the power of a well-delivered presentation. It's an opportunity to demonstrate your knowledge, passion, and commitment to your field. But great presentations don't just happen – they involve strategic preparation, enthusiastic delivery, and the effective use of visuals to support and enhance your narrative.

11.6. Communication in a Digital Age

In today's digital age, learning to navigate virtual meetings and emails are an indispensable part of your toolkit. Invest time in learning the apps and software for virtual communication. Pay attention to email etiquette, write clearly and succinctly, use bullet points when necessary, and always ensure your messages elicit the right response.

11.7. Cultural Sensitivity in Communication

In an increasingly global world, cultural sensitivity is a must. Remember that what feels 'right' in your culture may not necessarily resonate in another. Recognizing nuances in different cultures, especially in indirect communication styles, will go a long way in easing your cross-cultural collaborations.

The advancement of your career depends significantly on effective communication. We believe that playing your cards right in this area will not only shine a light on your abilities and dedication but will also foster beneficial relationships in your professional sphere, making way for a brighter future. In the final summation, always be open to learning and improving. As you apply these strategies, learn from your experiences, course-correct when necessary, and never stop refining your communication skills. With a sound approach and dedicated efforts, you have the power to shape your career trajectory just the way you want it.

www.ingramcontent.com/pod-product-compliance
Lightning Source LLC
Chambersburg PA
CBHW062312290526
45794CB00006B/2766